Stories of Mahishasuramardini & Post Mahabharata Battle

Apurba Chakraboty

Qurate
quratebooks.com

Stories of Mahishasuramardini & Post Mahabharata Battle
Apurba Chakraborty

Published by Qurate Books Pvt. Ltd.

Published in 2023

ISBN: 978-93-58980-01-1

Qurate Books Pvt. Ltd.
Goa 403523, India
www.quratebooks.com
Tel: 1800-210-6527, Email: info@quratebooks.com

*This holy book is dedicated to the present
as well as the upcoming generation &
the successors in future &
to enrich their knowledge with our eternal
ancient past.*

The courtesy for this book is Markandeya Purana & Vyasdeva's Mahabharata.

Reference

- For Mahishasurarardini from Markandeya Purana.
- The story of the Post Mahabharata battle is from Mahabharata by Vyas Deva.

Preface for the First Edition

This is a spontaneous attempt to present the stories of Mahishasuramardini & the story of the post-Mahabharata battle from Markandeya Purana and Mahabharata.

The story of Mahishasuramardini attracted me because it tells about the strength of women's power & savior of creation from evil and the Post Mahabharata stories tell about the ultimate destination of mortal life. The moral of both stories that ego is the enemy which needs to be destroyed to attain the ultimate success & peace.

Part One

Mahishasuramardini

CHAPTER - ONE

About the Sage Markandeya

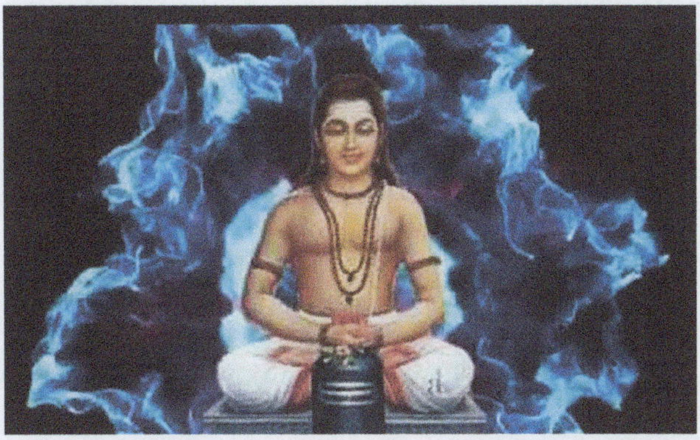

Sage Markandeya was a student of Lord Bramha and he originated from Hindu tradition born in the clan of the great Sage Vrigu. Sage Markandeya achieved his education by performing forceful religious practices and worshipping Brahm Kall.

He used to consider his worship as superior to the others. His concentration & chanting of verses would reach Brahmaloka.

There are in all three true experiences described in Mrkandeya Purana that show some light over the wrong religious practices where the three reasons for the continuous rotation & they couldn't end the endless cycle of birth and death.

Markandeya is closely associated with both Lord Shiva & Lord Vishnu. As Shiva being the destroyer of evil grants him life, and

Vishnu is the preserver of the good grants Markandeya the power to visualize the universe that goes through the cycle of birth & death. Markandeya is immortal and he knows more stories than anyone else who is alive at the moment in time. It is said that Markandeya have witnessed gods, kings, and sages in every period of humanity.

The story of Mahishasuramardini is written in the Devi Mahatmya, literally "glorification or praises of the Goddess", constitutes chapters 81 to 93 of the Markandeya Purana. It is the primary bhakti text of those who revere Durga or Chandi as the Shakti or source of Power.

The original version of Markandeya Purana was composed by Sage Markandeya near the holy river Narmada. In Markandeya Purana this is described as Devi Mahatmya.

CHAPTER -TWO

The Story Behind the Birth of Mahishasura

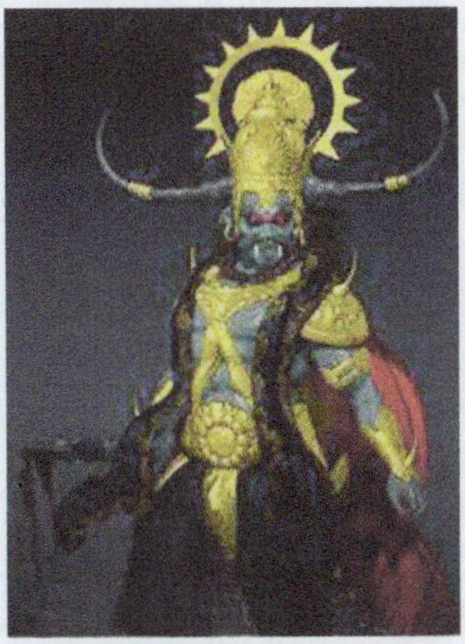

According to Puranas Rambha & Karambha, the two Asura brothers did penance for the blessing of having children. Rambha and Karambha meditated u pon Malavanta Yaksa. The former brother was seated at the center of the live fires and the latter was standing in the water of a lake. Then the king of Gods Indra observed this and decided to kill them.

First, in the form of a crocodile, he dragged Karambha away by the feet and killed him by drowning him. Then Indra went after Rmbha to kill him but was rescued by the Agni Deva. Being angry at the death of his brother Rambha decided to cut off his head and offer it as sacrifice. When he was about to do so Agni Deva appeared before him and told him that suicide is more worse than killing others and is considered as a great sin and he promised to grant him whatever he desires. Listening to this Rambha requested Agni Deva for a son more powerful than him who would conquer the three worlds and not be defeated even by the Gods and the Asuras. Rambha further desired that his son to be as powerful as Vayu, exceptionally handsome and skilled in archery. The Agno Deva blessed Rambha that he would have as desired a son by the woman whom he coveted.

On his easy back to home, Rambha saw a beautiful she buffalo named 'Mahishi' which he married. He took the she buffalo which got pregnant by him. He takes her to Patala to protect her from the attack by other buffalos. One day another buffalo felt a passion for Rambha's wife and in the fight that Rambha was killed by impaling him with his horns. Later the water buffalo was killed by Rambha's soldiers. Rambha's wife died in his funeral pyre by jumping into it.

It was from the centre of the fire that the very powerful Mahishasura was born. Rambha also rose from the fire with the name Raktabija along with his brother Mahishasura. This is a story of rebirth where Rambha was reborn as Raktabija the army Commander of Sumbha and Nisumbha.

Secured from Lord Shiva a blessing according to which if one drop of blood from his body fell on the battlefield number of Raktabijas would arise from the blood and fight with the enemies. Each of these Raktabijas would also be like the others in the matter of strength, form and weapons.

When Kaushiki was sent to crush the growing power of these two demon brothers she had to face the stiffest opposition from Raktabija. Kaushiki then took the form of Maha Kali and licked off the blood before they touched the ground. This way Raktabija was defeated and killed.

CHAPTER- THREE

Mahishashura get the Blessing from Lord Bramha

The word Mahis hasura is a Sanskrit word composed of Mahisha means buffalo and Asura means demon translated to Buffalo Demon. Mahishasura was the great-grandson of Brahmashi Kashyapa. As an Asura Mahishasura announced war against the Gods as the Gods and Asuras had all time conflict.

Mahishasura started meditating with the hope of blessing from Lord Bramha the supreme creator. He pleased with his long years of hard penance the Lord Bramha.

The Lord of Creation was pleased & agreed to grant him a boon.

Then the Asura king Mahishasura pleaded for immortality with the condition that the superpower demon Mahishasura only could be defeated by a woman & no menfolk could stand victorious against him.

CHAPTER-FOUR

Creation of Mahashakti

The most ferocious and brutal demon of all time Mahishasura harassed and subdued King Indra and all the other gods which includes Surya Dev a, Agni Deva, Pavan Deva, Yama Deva, Varuna Deva etc. And he occupied the throne of the heaven.His cruel acts created terror among the helpless sages and human beings.There was endless torture what they were subjected to. They were very much worried about their future. They have lost the hope and searching for a way out to get rid of Mahishasura.

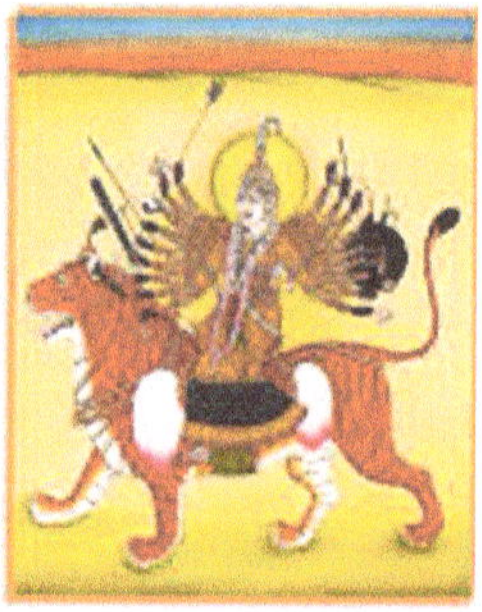

When there was no alternative they went to the Tripower means Bramha, Vishnu & Maheswar the gods for creation, stability & destruction.

Listening to the tortures from the harassed and frightened gods who fled from heaven the three Powers got so angry that their eyebrows emitted massive fires of fury which got combined as a huge Fire mountain into which the individual energies of all the gods headed by the King of Gods Indra got merged also.

The form of Maha Devi was thus materialised creating a luminous face with the combination of Powers in a formidal feminine form.

CHAPTER -FIVE

The Empowerment of Maha Shakti

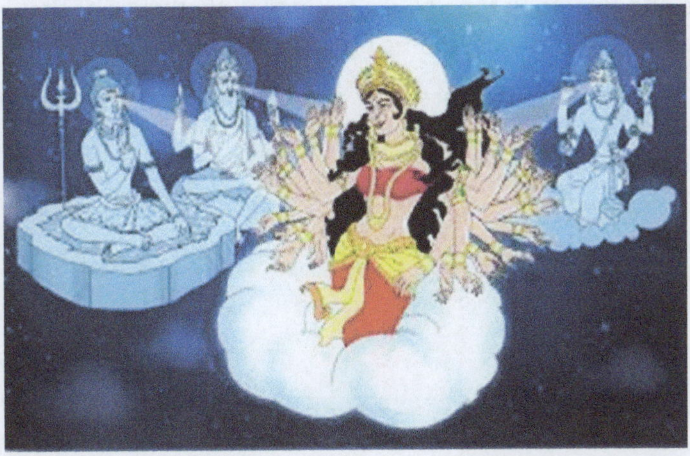

Yama's power created her hair, Vishnu's power provided her arms, Chandra's radiance gave sparkling jewels, Indra contributed the belly, Varuna's powers created thighs, Prithvi the rear, Brahma contributed the feet, Surya provided the fingers of the feet, Vasuganas contributed hand fingers, Kubera's Tejas created the nose, Prajapati's energy provided the teeth, Pavaka created her three eyes, both the Sadhyas gave away the mid-portion of eyebrows & Vayu supplied the Devis ears, then Mahadeva contributed his Shula from his own, Vishnu gave away a disc horn out of his disc,

Varuna gave a Shankha, Agni his Shakti, Vayu his Dhanus with powerful arrows, Indra gave his Vajra and a bell from Iravata, Yama gave his Kaldanda, Varuna a Pasha, Daksha Prajapati gave Akshaya Maala, Brahma his Kamandalu means water vessel, Surya supplied his rays into Maha Devi's skin pores, Kaal gave away his Sword, Samudra Deva contributed Pure Pearls, Shining Clothes, Valuable chudamani, Precious ear rings and bangles, Moon gave away Shoulder ornaments, necklaces and finger rings, Kavacha(Armour), Himalaya provided the carrier Lion and similarly all the other devas gifted various items of their valuable possessions. When suddenly there was a bewilde ring roar of a Lion's resound the whole universe trembled & felt that it was the end of the creation.

Mahishashura and his followers got shivered with unprecedented noise and they took time to realise indeed that was not the end of the creation but the beginning of the great battle.

Maha Devi's radiance spreaded all over the directions when her thousand arms came into flashes of mercurial actions.

CHAPTER-SIX

The Fierce Battle Between Devi Chandika & Mahishasura

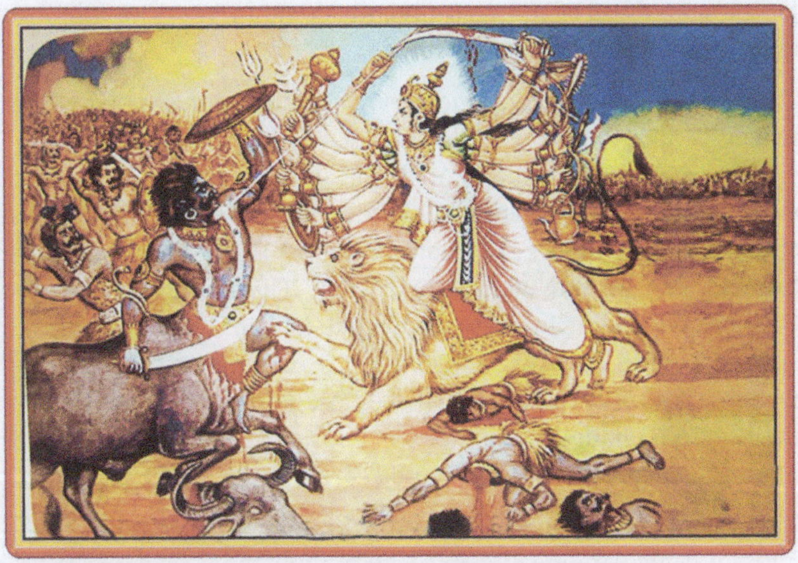

Lord Vishnu gave her the name of Goddess Chandika. She rides on a lion her vehicle that Ki ng Himavan had given her. And the Gods prayed to her to destroy the evil demon Mahishasura.

As the goddess descended on earth the skies and the seas trembled. The terrified demon King Mahishasura ordered his enormous army to attack the one who makes the storming sound. Goddess Chandrika on her lion saw the uncountable army of demons.

Ugrasencame with sixty thousand chariots, Chixsura came with one million horsemen, Vidhan came with one hundred soldiers & Vaskaal came with uncounted demons. The demons of Mahishasura saw Devi Chandika & & the voice of her roar, the twang of her bow string echoed al through the heavens to hell, the feet to the nether world, the crown kissing the skies & a thousand hands filled with weapons filled the sky in all the directions.

The furious battle starts with Devi Chandika and the demons attacking each other with opposite weapons. All the bad weapons each demon warrior used all of the opposite weapons of Devi Chandika strike the demon weapon and break. This went on for quite some time.The demons then attacked her with a rain of arrows. About one hundred arrows flew up in the sky. Devi Chandika used the same number of arrows & then the demon arrows were broken by Devi Chadika's opposite arrows.

This went fr quite some time. Devi Chandika almost used all her weapons like the trident, mace, discus, arrow, shield, sword, scimitar, battle-axe, weapon made out of thorns spear, longsword, vajra, spade, baton, beating stick, thunderbolt and javelin. Which stabbed the demons really hard. Some of them were beheaded, bruised, and beaten with beating stick. The demons fought the Goddess with their finest weapons like javelins, daggers, scythes, spears, pestles, swords, and battle-axe but all of those demon weapons have been broken to pieces and nooses has been flung at the Goddess Chandika. Counter weapons of demons by raining her own weapons which she has rained earlier.

The lion of Devi Chandika himself, with his paws scratching them with his claws, ripping of their heads making them armless, legless, headless, choking them,stabbing their chests, drinking their blood, breaking their bones, breaking their necks, twisting their hands and legs, swinging them away and doing more worse things to the demons.

Devi Chandika can see that her lion was a great demon-fighting warrior and she congratulated him. Although there were still an army of one thousand demon soldiers and the number of demons. Devi Chandika created an equal number of male and female warriors.

They were all holding weapons like a trident, mace, discus, arrow, shield, sword, scimitar, battle-axe, a weapon made out of thrones, spear, long sword, vajra, spade, baton, beating stick, thunderbolt and javelin etc. The warriors of Devi Chandika managed to fight with the rest of the endless demon army of Ugrasen,Vashkaal, Chixsura, and Vidhan. As a celebration, Devi Chandika's army started dancing, singing, and playing the drums, flutes, sitars, and many more. Devi Chandika pinned down demons with her weapons like trident,mace,sword and spear.

Devi Chandika killed them by ringing her strong mighty bell and dragged some of them with her noose. Many were beheaded by the Goddess and got smashed by her mighty mace. Some got crushed by pestle and their chests were torn by the Goddess's trident. Many got pierced by the Goddess's arrows and breathed their last breath. Many decapitated demons rose & started dancing to the beats of the musical instruments played by the Goddess's soldiers. Many decapitated demons yelled and again fought the Devi Chandika with their finest weapons.

Heaps of the corpses of the demons, slain elephants, horses, wrecked chariots, and river of demon's blood flowed. As fire reduced twigs and leaves into ashes & similarly Devi Chandika destroyed the imperial army of Mahishasura with the help of her lion within minutes. All Gods, saints, sages, celestial beings, yakshas, men, women & children paid gratitude to Goddess Chandika for the killing of Mahishasur's demon army. Rest seventeen demon men of Mahishasura, Chixsura, Chamar, Ugrasen, Upal, Vidat, Vidhan, Ugravirya, Tamra, Trinetra, Udugrasura, Karalasura, Vashkaal, Durdhara, Mahahanu, Ugrasya, Bakalasura, Udyatarasura, Vilaxa & Durmukh were all generals. Devi Chandika killed all the seventeen generals with her weapon made out of thorns, spear, longsword, vajra, spade, baton, beating stick, javelin, trident, mace, sword, scimitar, arrow, thunderbolt and battleaxe which beheaded them, and were stabbed them crucially.

For her counterattacks, she had managed to dispatch the four-fold demon infantries with her lion and other demons. She sucked out of the remaining life of the demons by blowing them in a single strike.

She rain arrows at Udagra, Asilom, Parivarita,Virhalax & Vaskalasura as drives of the countless number of chariots. Now Mahishasura was the last demon to enter the battlefield. He fought Devi Chandika with his different weapons once again all the bad weapons he used all of the opposite weapons of Devi Chandrika to strike the demon weapon and then breaks. This went on for quite some time. The demon then attacked her with a rain of arrows.

About one hundred arrows flew up in the sky. Devi Chandika used the similar number of arrows and then the demon arrows were broken by Devi Chandika's opposite arrows. Again this continued for quite some time. After that, he kept changing so many forms like lion, warrior, buffalo, elephant, etc. Devi Chandika killed his various forms by using scimitar, sword, etc. Later Mahishasura again obtained the form of a buffalo and attacked Devi Chandika with trees, rocks, boulders & mountains. But Devi Chandika had managed to destroy them all.

At last, the Goddess drank water from her cup and announced to Mahishasura that she will kill him. Devi Chandika this time managed to trample the buffalo with her lion. Mahishasura comes out of the buffalo's mouth & he tried to kill the Goddess with his sword. Devi Chandika stabbed his body with her trident.

All the Gods, saints, sages, celestial beings, yakshas, yakshinis, men. women & children paid gratitude and started the prayer ritual to her.

We greet her who is present in the form of wealth in the houses of the virtuous and who disappears in the form of poverty in the residences of the vily and the vicious, who is present with those who are well read and of a clean conscience as also a practitioner of diligence, composure & modesty. How are we competent to describe your Achintya Rupa means evergreen form?

Devas further exclaimed "Oh Maha Devi you are the Adya Prakruti devoid of Vikaras of Satva, Raja, and Tamo gunantimka and thus the cause of the universe. Even Vishnu and Mahadeva who are subject to realise your indifferences. You are the nucleus of all the materialistic manifestations.

They prayed by chanting "Devi you have killed all the enemies and saved the Treeokas, bestowed heaven to them all and demolished our fears & saved us do protect us with your Shula, Khadga, Ghanta, Dhanush and it's tankara or sound.

Chandika Eswari do protect us by circling our East, West, South & North directions.

Highly pleased by the above commendations of the gods and sages Maha Devi gave an opportunity to them to ask for blessings and they said politely that after the killing of Mahishasura, they had no further requests to make except that she should kindly respond as and when exigencies might arise in future & she said "Tathastu" which means "Be it so".

CHAPTER-SEVEN

The Story Behind the Name Mahishur or Mysuru Presently Karnataka

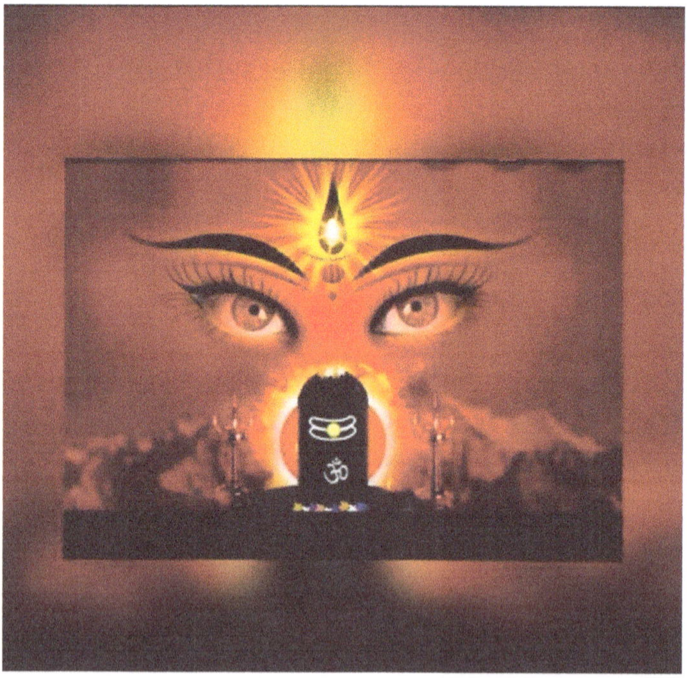

As per the Devi Purana Mysuru was ruled by the demon King Mah ishasura. He was a buffalo headed monster. Responding to the pleading of the Gods, saints, sages, and celestial bodies to save them from the torture & harassment by the demon the Goddess Parvathi took birth as Chamundeshwari to kill the monster. The killing spot of the demon King was on the top of Chamunda hill and the city have the names Chamunda hill and Mysuru.

The word Mysuru is a corrupted version of Mysooru which originated from the word Mahishur meaning the town of Mahishasuru in Kannada.

A different myth is also there where the most popular legend is Mysore gets its name from Mahishasuramardini a manifestation of goddess Durga. The buffalo-headed demon Mahishasura states the regional tradition had terrified the local population. It is believed that the goddess Chamundeshwari killed Mahishasura on the top of the Chamundi Hills. The spot was built as the Chamudeshwari temple in Mysuru an event that is celebrated every year as Navaratri and Mysuru Dassera.

CHAPTER -EIGHT

About Navaratri Festival Celebrated all over the Country

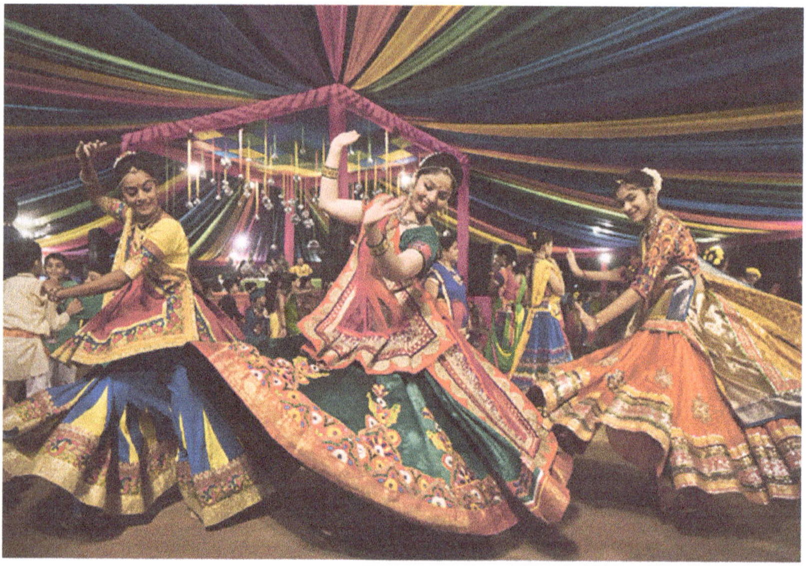

Navaratri is a Hindu festival celebrated every year in honour of the Goddess Durga who is the Adi Shakti in the month of Ashwin(September/October) and in the month of Chaitra(March/April). Navaratri span over nine nights & ten days. The battle to kill Mahishasura lasted for nine days.

To mark the win over evil power and to honur women's empowerment Navaratri observed in different parts of India. In practice, this is a post-monsoon autumn festival called Sharad Navaratri.

The festival is associated with the battle of Devi Yiddha that took place between Durga and the demon king Mahishasura. To celebrate the victory of good over the evil power. All these days are solely dedicated to Mother Durga and her nine forms known as Navadurga. Each day is related to an incarnation of the goddess.

The greatness of each day is illustrated here as follows:-

Day One- Shailaputri

Pratipada is the first day which is related to the form Shailaputri means daughter of mountain an incarnation of Parvati. This is the form of Devi Durga is worshipped as the daughter of Himavan the guardian god of the Himalayas. She is depicted as riding the bull Nandi with a trident in her right hand and lotus in her left hand. Shailaputri is considered the direct incarnation of Mahakali. She as well considered to be a reincarnation of Sati & is also known as Hemavati.

Day Two-Brahmacharini

The goddess Brahmacharini is another incarnation of Parvati is worshipped in this form.

Parvati became Yogini her unmarried self. Brahmacharini is worshipped for moksha and endowment of peace and prosperity.

Day Three-Chandraghanta

The third auspicious day is dedicated for the worship of Chandraghanta the name derived from the fact that after marrying Lord Shiva Parvati adorned her forehead with half moon. She is the embodiment of beauty and is also symbol of bravery.

Day Four-Kushmanda

On the fourth day, Goddess Kushmanda is worshipped. Believed that the creative power of the universe, Kushmanda is associated with the endowment of vegetation on earth.

Day Five -Skandamata

On the fifth day, the goddess Skandamata is worshipped who is the mother of Skanda alias Kartikkeya. This symbolises the transforming strength of a mother when her child is confronted with danger.

Day Six-Katyay ani

Born to sage Kayan she is the incarnation of Durga & is shown to exhibit courage which is symbolized by the red colour. She is known as the warrior goddess. She is considered one of the most violent forms of Devi Maha Shakti is observed on this day starting of Shardiya Durga Puja.

Day Seven-Kaala ratri

This form is considered the most ferocious form of the Goddess Durga. Kaalaratri is reversed on Saptami. It is believed that Parvati removed her pale skin to kill the demons Sumbha & Nisumbha. The goddess is worshipped on Saptami. In eastern India Maha Saptami on this day.

Day Eight-Mahagauri

This form of Mahagauri symbolizes intelligence and peace.It is believed when Kaalaratri took a bath in the holy river Ganges she gained a warmer complexion.

She is worshipped on Maha Ashtami in eastern India. Maha Ashtami is observed on this day and starts with Pushpanjali, Kumari Puja etc. It is a very important tithi & is considered the birthday of Mahishasura Mardini form of the Devi Chandika.

Day Nine-Siddhidatri

This is the last day of the celebration also known as Navami. People pray to Siddhidartri sitting on a lotus & she is believed to possess and bestows all types of Siddhis. Here she is known as Mahalaxmi. Siddhidatri is Parvati the wife of Lord Shiva.

As per Vedic scriptures Lord Shiva attained all the Siddhis by worshipping this Goddess.

All over India tools & weapons are worshipped in a ritual called Ayudha Puja.

CHAPTER-NINE

The Majesty of the Goddess

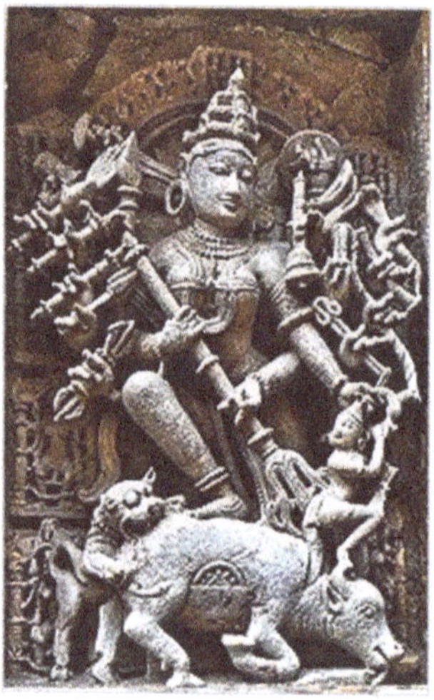

This is literally the glorification and praise of the great Goddess who is the moth er of the creation, the Adishakti. This constitutes from chapter eighty-one to chapter ninety-three of the Markandeya Purana. It is titled as Sapstasati or Chandi mahatmya. Most popular in West Bengal & Odisha the eastern provinces of India.

This greatness of the Goddess or Devi Mahatmya starts with the legendary King Suratha, who was defeated in the battle and exiled & Samadhi who was a merchant and was driven away by his wives & children owing to his wealth.

They both met once in the forest. Nevertheless asserts King Suratha & merchant Samadhi realised that they both care about the welfare of those who drove them out.

They were surprised then that why they still care for them. Then they met the sage Sumedha and asked him to explain the fallacy. The sage Sumedha answered that this is the nature of existence. Just watch hungry birds who collect seeds and despite being hungry those birds drop the seeds into the beaks of their babies. This is the power of the Goddess, her manifestation in nature and everywhere one who empowers attachments, yet also empowers release, asserts.

Then King Suratha and Samadhi desired to know more about the Goddess. The sage then described Devi Mahatmya which is a part of Markandeya Purana and tells in detail about the Goddess with theological & philosophical premises focussed as described above.

Part Two

Stories of Post-Mahabharata Battle

CHAPTER -ONE

Post Events after the Great Battle of Kurukshetra

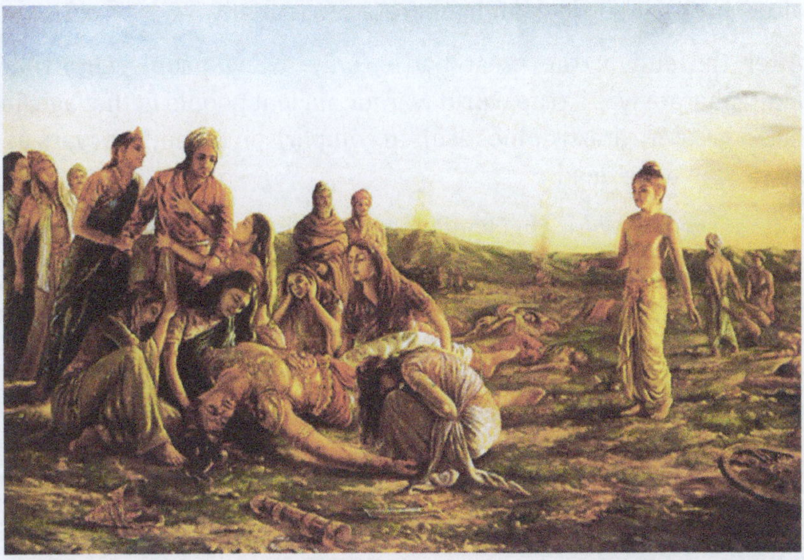

This is a matter of fact that no one illustrated to us what happened after the wa r of Mahabharata as it described in detail about the battle from every nook and corner.

Obviously, Mahabharata is the greatest epic till date ever written. The epic has a deep-rooted impact on Indian culture, customs & even the way people conduct themselves at present. The stories also have momentum in understanding what is morally wrong and correct in the Indian tradition.

Although most of the knowledge people have about Mahabharata is by reading and analyzing the reality but through fictitious representation. And the attraction of the stories of Mahabharata ends with the end of the Kurukshetra battle. What happened after the great battle in the great epic is still very little came to light.

What happened after the Mahabharata battle which shaped culturally and philosophically the Indian culture that we are aware of presently. The knowledge of Mahabharata is incomplete without knowing the events after the Kurukshetra battle.

Now let us go through one after another incident that happened after the great battle of Mahabharata sequentially.

After the end of the great battle, only a few people survived. Mahabharata was a true world war for ancient people in that age. It had a greater catastrophic result in comparison to modern wars as all people were dead.

The survivors were the Pandavas with their wives and mother Kunti. Then Dhritarashtra and his wife Gandhari., Sri Krishna, Satyaki & Yuyutsu. The rest other names were Ashwathama the son of Dronacharya, Kritavarma who was a Vrishni warrior Kripacharya the teacher of Pandavas & Kauravas & the last name was Vrishaketu the son of the great warrior Karna. This was the scenario after the great war of Mahabharata.

CHAPTER-TWO

Arjuna Lost Most of his Powers

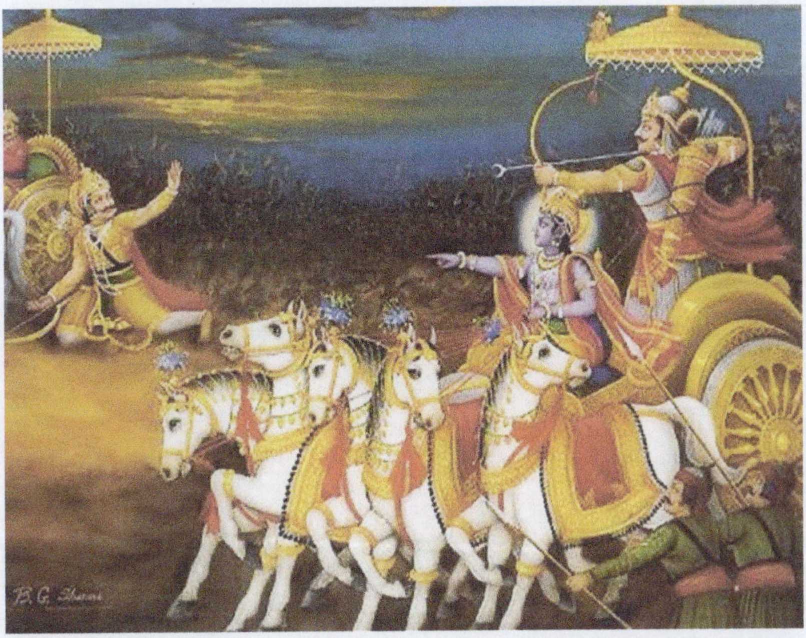

Next important outcome after the great battle the all-time greatest warrior Arjuna lost most of the powers he had. Logically Arjuna was one of the central characters and bravest warriors in the Kurukshetra battlefield of Mahabharata. It was told that the extraordinary power Arjuna possessed was to fight in favour of the Dharma means Dharma Yudh.

However, everything drastically changed after the Kurukshetra battle ended. Arjuna lost almost all his power even to the extent that he was not able to fight a number of ordinary thieves who tried to kidnap Lord Krishna's wife.

CHAPTER-THREE

Yudhisthira's Coronation as the Crown King

As per traditional practice, the eldest son of Pandu passed to the throne. It was followed as per the Hindu customs the eldest son becomes the king of the throne of Hastinapur. Although being a truly noble man Yudhisthira offer his uncle Dhritarashtra to remain on the throne. Dhritarashtra however doesn't agree and leaves the throne.

CHAPTER-FOUR

Rehabilitation for the Widows of Kaurava Martyrs

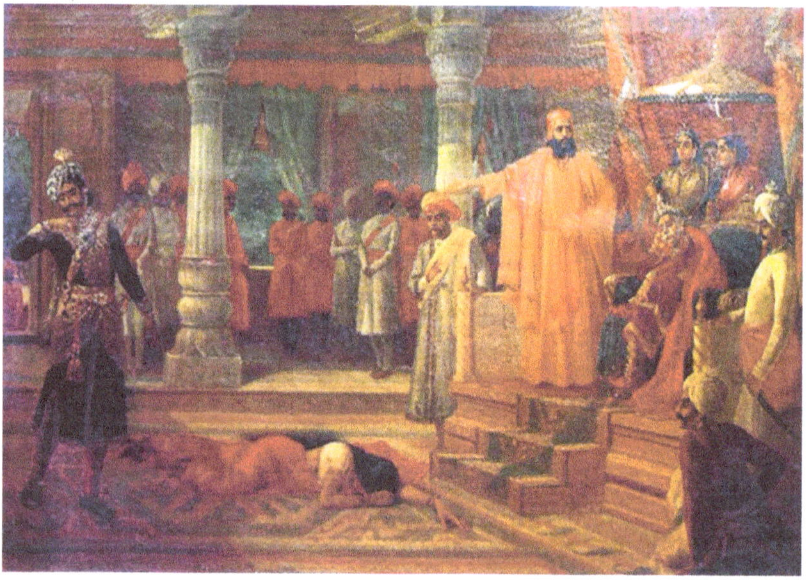

A council of women was formed by Draupadi consisting of all the war widows. The council looks after their rehabilitation and assured that everyone could support their families financially by providing them with dignified work possibilities.

The women's council gave respectable positions to Kaurava's widows in the palace of the Pandavas.

CHAPTER-FIVE

Gandhari's Curse to Sri Krishna

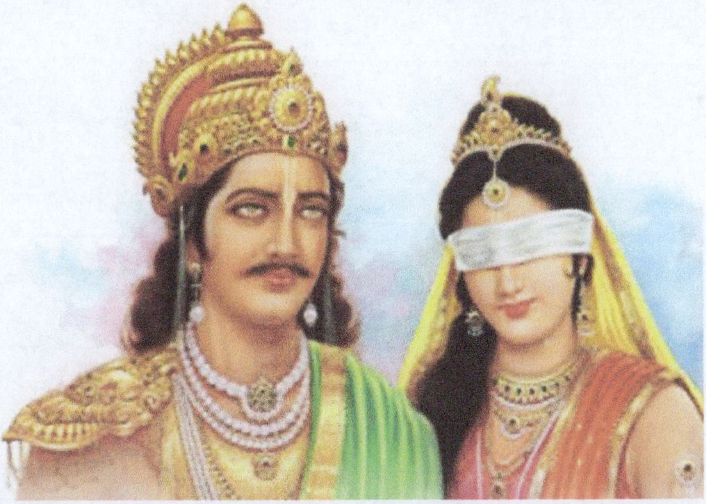

Gandhari got very angry and held Sri Krishna responsible on seeing her sons lying dead in the battlefield and their bodies were mutilated by carnivorous worms. The result was she cursed Sri Krishna and told him "You will witness your kinsmen dying in front of you as I have seen my sons dying on the battlefield."

Gandhari's curse to Sri Krishna took thirty-six years to materialize which approached the end of Lord Sri Krishna and his clan Yadava of Dwarka a period during which the Pandavas were in power. The violence in the city of Dwarka started with Yadavas killing each other. Mausala Parva states about Sri Krishna's death in the thirty-sixth year, which took place as the result of an arrow shot him mistakenly by Jara and appears before him in the image of Lord Vishnu. This event describes the beginning of Kaliyuga which we know at present.

CHAPTER-SIX

Gandhari & Dhritarasra Leave for Penance as Bhim Criticize them

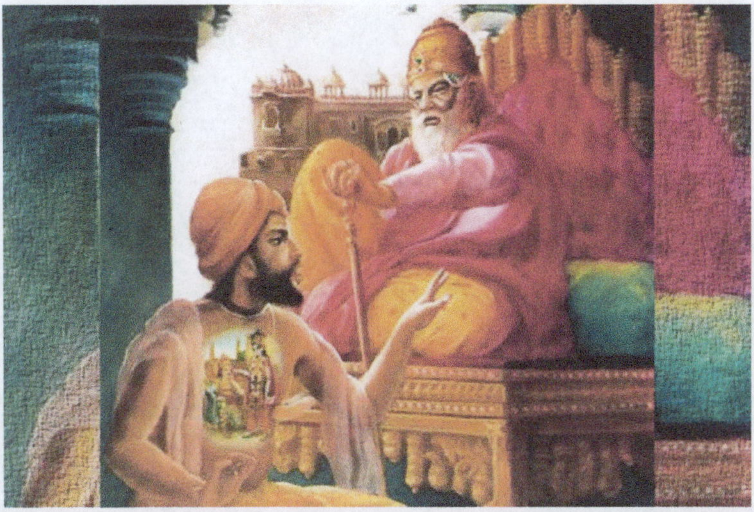

Perfor ming the last rituals of their sons and other relatives indulging in severe penance Gandhari and Dritarastra were alive for two years. In some versions of Mahabharata, it was told that middle Pandav Bhim used to criticize the couple. Owing to this reason they left the kingdom for penance in the forest. Kunti and Sanjay also accompanied Dhritarashtra & Gandhari. Dhritarashtra and the other three die in a forest fire in meditating conditions from which they could have escaped but their choice was to die peacefully.

CHAPTER-SEVEN

The Pandavas Left Hastinapur to Final Journey

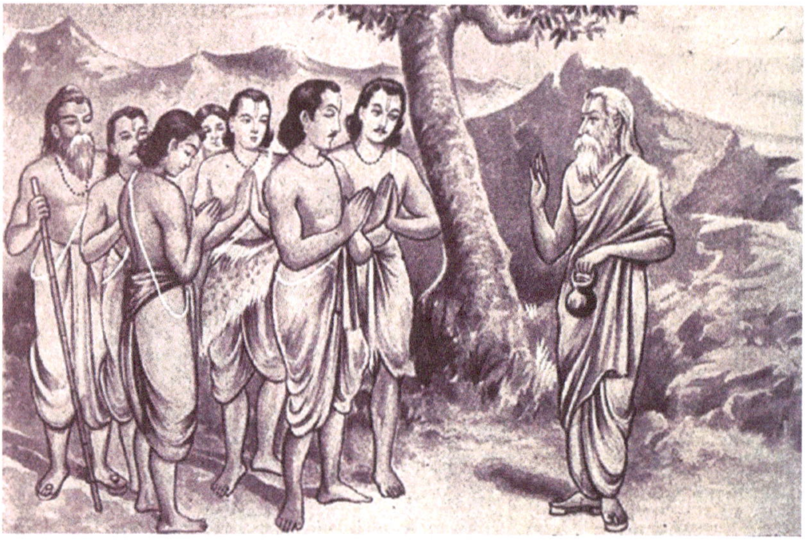

The Pandavas left Hastinapur & mortal life on the way to their final journey to heaven from the Himalayas. Veda Vyas advised the Pandavas that they have served the purpose of their life and that now they should leave for their final towards the Himalayas. The Pandavas with their wife Draupadi then leave their kingdom Hastinapur. All along their journey a dog was befriended with them.

The Pandavas reach the South first towards the sea & perform rituals there. Then near the sea, Agni Deva appeared before them. He told to Arjuna that the bow he was holding is a powerful one & it was sent to him by the Gods to fight the evil to establish truth and faith. As the purpose has been achieved Arjuna too has to leave off the duties as a Commander in Chief.

So the Agni Deva told Arjuna to return his bow named "Gandib" to him. Accordingly, Arjuna returned his bow saying "Oh Deva,I agree that I have fulfilled your expectations. Now that we have to leave the mortal world so I don't find any reason to keep the bow with me."With this, he returned his bow to the Agni Deva.

They move from south to southwest and visited so many places, Ashrams & from there they proceed further to Dwarka. The unique & glorious city like that was no more there. The Pandavas see the city was flooded and from the land, Sri Krshna's palace standing among the waters was very much visible.

The Pandavas were sad at the sight of such a beautiful city submerged in seawater. Then they turned north and halted at Rishikesh. From there they again started their journey for the Himalayas. Their target was to cross Mount Meru and reach heaven.

CHAPTER-EIGHT

When Climbing the Himalayas

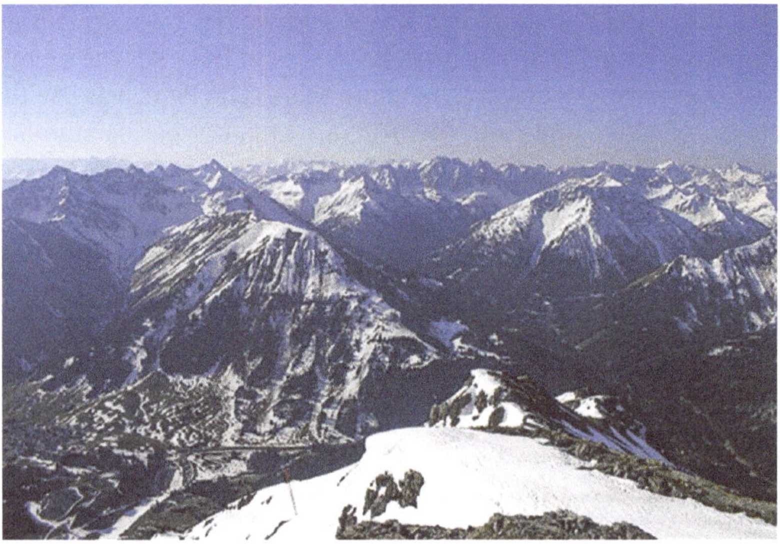

While climbing the Himalayas four Pandavas and Draupadi fall & die but only Yudhishthira survives and continued his journey towards heaven. During the journey, a d og was friendly with them and accompanied the Pandavas for the entire journey. Draupadi was the first one to fall down while ascending the Himalayas followed by Sahadeva, Nakula, Arjuna & lastly Bhima. Yudhishthira gave the explanation of their falling due to various sins committed during their lifetime. In this manner, Yudhishthira and the dog continued on their ascent toward heaven.

CHAPTER-NINE

The Final Test of Yudhishthira

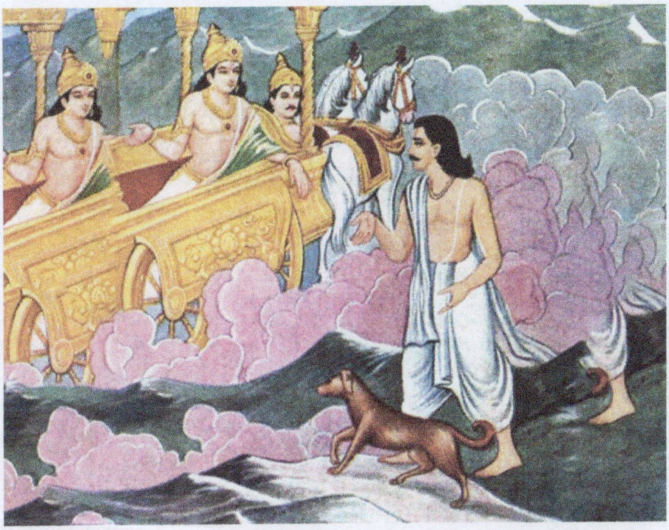

As soon as Yudhishthira and the dog climb the Himalayas Lord Indra the King of Gods appeared before him on his chariot and asked Yudhishthira to come to heaven along with him.

But Yudhisthira insisted Lord Indra to allow the dog to be with him. But Lord Indra didn't agree to keep the request but Yudhishthira was very much rigid about his logic. Later Yudhishthira realized that the dog was the Dharma in the form of a dog only. Dharma was surprised by Yudhishthira's virtues & appreciate him eventually he entered Lord Indra's chariot towards heaven with Yudhishthira.